Fondues

Antje Grüner

Fondue – a total delight

Whether you are with friends or your family,
a fondue evening always promises a few
convivial hours. Hosts can sit at the
table as comfortably as their guests and entertain
them in a relaxed way, for all the ingredients
are set ready, everyone cooks their own and
helps themselves to the accompaniments:
sauces, dips, chutneys, fresh salads and crisp
bread. It is a thoroughly enjoyable occasion
which gives pleasure to all ages.

AURA

CONTENTS

What is a fondue?

Originally the word fondue came from *fromage fondu*, meaning melted cheese. Swiss mountain peasants made a virtue of necessity and dipped their bread in melted cheese so that they could enjoy an inexpensive and nourishing warm meal and, in the process, they invented the national dish of Switzerland, the cheese fondue. For many years now, it has been a popular dish far beyond the frontiers of its native country. Since then, the word fondue has come to be used for a variety of different kinds of cooking in a pan at the dining table, although we still distinguish between cheese, oil and stock fondues.

The *fondue bourguignonne*, which has now become as popular as the cheese fondue, did not originate in Burgundy and nor is it prepared with red wine. Was it the result of creativity, lack of time or simply laziness on the part of a cook on the shores of Lake Geneva? He offered his guests raw meat, a selection of sauces and side dishes and a pan containing hot oil on the table and wished them a good appetite. Each guest could assemble their own meal in any way they pleased. In this way the meat fondue was invented.

With the cooking pots or 'fire-pots' used in Asian cookery, another very popular fondue came on to our menus. This fondue is not cooked in oil, but in stock. It is easy to prepare and, in addition, is extremely healthy.

Essential equipment – the fondue pan

Whatever type of fondue you choose, you need to use the right type of pan for it. This is always placed on the table on a *réchaud*, a stand with a burner underneath. For cheese fondues, a *caquelon*, a specially designed ceramic pan with a thick handle, is used. It is fairly flat and wide, approximately 18–20 cm/7–8 inches in diameter. This is necessary because you need plenty of room to stir the fondue from time to time. Enamelled cast iron pans with a similar diameter are also suitable.

The pan used for an oil fondue is usually smaller (about 18 cm/7 inches in diameter) and taller, sometimes narrowing towards the top. It is made of stainless steel, enamelled steel, cast iron or stainless copper. Many of these pans have a splash-guard with a hanger for the fondue forks. This is a useful arrangement because it prevents the forks from getting into a muddle during cooking and keeps things in order. Also available are rather expensive copper-based fondue pans, which can also be used for conventional cooking.

There are even showpiece combination fondue sets, which include sauce bowls, as well as the basic equipment.

Classically for the stock-based fondue, a very special pan is used, the Mongolian 'fire-pot', which is made of copper, brass or aluminium. It has a chimney in the middle, under which a charcoal fire glows and heats the stock. Other models are heated with a *réchaud* or by electricity. The size of the pan – about 30 cm/12 inches in diameter – is large enough for the special fondue scoops and a 'fire-pot' contains about 2–2.5 litres/3^1/$_2$–4^1/$_4$ pints of stock. Enthusiasts for stock-based fondues will already know the value of this 'fire-pot'. Newcomers can use a wide, shallow saucepan until they decide that stock-based fondues are so delicious it is worth investing in a 'fire-pot'.

A *réchaud* is indispensable. Safety burners that use a fuel-paste are now taking over from spirit burners, which can be a fire hazard. If you have an old spirit burner, you would be wise to look out for this new equipment and replace it.

A word about accessories – fondue forks, usually with two prongs, are necessary because they have very long stems. This makes it easy to spear the food to be cooked and to remove it from the fork when it is ready. Cheese fondue forks usually have three prongs. Normal table forks are not suitable and could cause injury. Fondue forks have differently coloured marks on the handles so that you can tell them apart when they are all in the pan together. When you lay the table, make sure every place setting has two forks with the same colour marks. Special fondue crockery usually consists of one large serving plate and about three smaller ones for the sauces and side dishes, but this is not at all essential.

Setting up

Obviously, it is sensible to put the stand and fondue pan in the centre of the table, so that no one has to stretch dangerously across it. It is also important that you set out the raw fondue ingredients and accompanying sauces on several different serving plates and in a number of bowls, so that everyone at the table can reach them comfortably. If you do not have enough small bowls and dishes for the sauces, you can serve them in attractive glasses, such as wide-brimmed champagne glasses or wine goblets.

Melting a cheese fondue

Of all good things, there are three that you must have to

hand for a delicious, savoury fondue: cheese, white wine and fresh, crusty bread.

<u>Ingredients</u>
The most important thing is to choose the cheese well. If possible, buy it fresh and unwrapped from a delicatessen or specialist cheese shop. The most suitable cheeses are hard and semi-hard cheeses with a minimum of 45 per cent fat content. Suitable kinds include Appenzeller, Bel Paese, Cheddar, Cheshire, Emmental, Gouda, Gruyère, Tilsit and Parmesan. The riper a cheese, the fuller its flavour. Mature cheeses tend to be stronger,

while young cheese has a mild taste. To obtain the best flavour, mix mature and ripe cheeses together. They do not have to be the same variety. Experiment with different combinations of your own favourite cheeses.

Choose a dry sparkling wine with a natural acidity. This is important to make the cheese melt evenly. As a safety net, have some lemon juice or vinegar to hand.

Before going into preparing the fondue, a word about what to serve with it – the bread. Traditionally, white bread, cut into bite-size pieces, is served. Sliced bread is not suitable because the slices are too thin and the texture is too floppy, so the bread cubes do not stay on the fork and fall into the fondue. A range of different breads, especially those with caraway, sesame or sunflower seeds, is tastier than plain white bread alone.

Preparation
Coarsely grate the cheese. Bring the wine to the boil in a fondue pan. Gradually, add the grated cheese, 30–45 ml/ 2–3 tablespoons at a time, stirring with a wooden spoon in rapid figure-of-eight movements until the cheese

has melted. Then add the next portion of cheese. Continue in this way, melting each addition completely, until the cheese is used up. Never stir round and round, as the cheese will go lumpy. You can thicken the fondue with cornflour mixed to a paste with cold water, then seasoned with pepper and freshly grated nutmeg.

The *fondue* has acquired the right consistency when the cheese will cover a bread cube in a creamy coating without dripping. Put the pan on the stand and adjust the flame so that it is high enough to keep the fondue bubbling gently.

With a cheese fondue, it is important to add the grated cheese in small quantities at a time and to ensure that it has melted completely before you add the next batch. Keep stirring the fondue in figure-of-eight movements until all the cheese has been added..

Handling
Spear a piece of bread with your fondue fork and dip it into the cheese. Revolve the fork gently and then lift it out. Eat straight from the fondue fork, but be careful because the melted cheese is very hot. It is best to wait a few seconds to allow it to cool slightly, so that you do not burn your mouth. A proper cheese fondue also contains a small glass of kirsch. This is an aid to digestion because melted cheese is heavy on the stomach. If you are particularly sensitive, you should not drink wine with the fondu, but tea instead.

Dropping bread cubes off your fork into the fondue pan is not considered acceptable. The traditional 'fine' for doing this is to drink a full glass of wine. However, this is likely to lead to even less control over the fondue fork and, in any case, too much wine is hardly safe in the circumstances.

Tips and tricks
• If the cheese fondue is too thin, add some more grated cheese, a little at a time, stirring constantly in figure-of-eight movements.
• If the cheese fondue is too thick, stir in a little lukewarm wine with a whisk.
• A 'little drop of something' gives a 'lift'. Besides kirsch, pear, plum or apple brandy are good additions to the mixture.
• To keep the cheese fondue creamy, stir it with a wooden spoon from time to time.
• Cheese fondue is very filling, so you can probably do

without a starter or dessert, which makes entertaining in this way easier, as well as fun.
• When all the fondue has been eaten, there will be a brown crust on the base of the fondue pan. This is a particularly delicious titbit.

Oil fondues – crispy fried delicacies

Frying in hot oil is, of course, a well-known cooking technique. The original, classic *fondue bourguignonne* pioneered the way to a whole series of new fondue creations with different kinds of meat, poultry, fish and other ingredients.

Ingredients

Whether you choose meat or fish, you must be absolutely sure to use first class ingredients. Probably the best meats are beef and pork fillets, but anything that can be fried quickly, such as steak, chicken breast, turkey breast and pork cutlets, is suitable. Use only filleted fish. Any variety with firm flesh, such as swordfish, tuna, salmon or salmon trout, is ideal. Many types of seafood, such as prawns and mussels are also suitable.

Cut the fish and meat into 2 cm/³/₄ inch cubes, so that they will become golden brown on the outside and tender and juicy inside. Chunks that are too small quickly dry out; those that are too large rapidly turn dark brown on the outside while remaining raw inside.

Any oil that can be brought to a high heat, such as corn, groundnut or sunflower, is

It is essential to use the right oil or fat for fondues – neutral-tasting vegetable oil, deep-frying fat or coconut oil.

suitable for frying. Do not use olive oil. Heat the oil in a saucepan first, then pour it into a fondue pan. It is important that the oil is really hot before the fondue ingredients are added to the pan. Adjust the burner to keep the oil hot, but do not overheat, as this will spoil the taste of the fondue and could be dangerous.

Handling

Spear one piece of meat at a time on the fondue fork and hold it in the hot oil. Test with the first piece, so that you get an idea how long it takes to cook. Then push it off with your table fork, sprinkle with salt and pepper and dip it in the sauce of your choice. Never eat directly from the fondue fork, as it would cause serious burns.

Tips and Tricks

• To tell if the oil is hot enough, put a chunk of white bread into the fondue pan. If it turns golden brown, the oil is ready.
• Pat meat and fish thoroughly dry with absorbent kitchen paper. This is particularly important if they have been marinated. Otherwise they will spit in the hot oil.
• Sauces and dips make seasoning superfluous. However, if you still want

to season your food with salt and pepper; add it after cooking, otherwise it makes for an unpleasant burnt taste.
• Do not put fondue pans in the dishwasher because they may spread a light film of oil over the other dishes.

Stock-based fondues – easy and low-calorie

Fondue chinoise or 'chrysanthemum fire-pot' are evocative names for a very ancient cooking method, which comes from Asia.

Instead of oil, the ingredients are cooked in stock. This is a fondue which is becoming increasingly popular in the West. This is not only because it is easily digestible and low-calorie, but because it is also particularly tasty. A stock-based fondue may contain not only meat or fish, but also a wealth of savoury vegetables. There are no limits to what the imagination can produce.

Stock and ingredients

Whether you are using meat or fish, the stock must never be too strongly flavoured because it will become even more concentrated during cooking. This is why the recipes always say a light stock. If you do not want to make the stock yourself, use a good ready-made one, which you should prepare using only half the quantity described in the packet instructions.

You will find a recipe for home-made chicken stock on page 14 and there is a fish stock in the recipe on page 32. A light chicken stock is also suitable for cooking fish. It is essential to use best-quality, fresh ingredients for the stock. Always strain the stock well so that it is as clear as possible.

Preparation

Take enough time for preparation because the ingredients have to be very finely sliced. A sharp knife makes the work easier. Put meat and fish in the freezer for 2–3 hours before slicing them. This makes it much easier to cut them into wafer-thin slices. You can also use a mechanical slicer or food processor, depending on the blades supplied. Always slice meat across the grain. Vegetables may be cut into thin slices or julienne strips.

Handling

Fondue scoops or baskets are virtually indispensable. You can buy one in a department store, Asian shops or Chinese supermarkets. The best way to cook the finely sliced ingredients is in a container of this sort.

Tips and tricks

• The stock should be gently simmering. If it is boiling too vigorously, it will quickly reduce and become too strong. If

For a stock-based fondue you need to slice the meat as thinly as possible. freeze the meat beforehand and, if possible, cut it with an electric slicer.

necessary, stir in more hot water to dilute it.
- Fresh herbs give the stock a delicious flavour.
- The concentrated stock is a delicacy, which you can serve at the end of the meal.
- Meat and fish can be cooked together in the stock without any problems.
- Prepare a strong stock. Freeze it in portions and heat it up diluted with water.
- A slightly less authentic way to cook this fondue is to use a wide saucepan instead of a 'fire-pot'.

Be careful of quality
It is important that beef and pork should have been be well hung. You can tell this by the dark colour of the meat. Beef

Most important for all types of fondue: the ingredients must always be absolutely fresh so that the fondue tastes really delicious. Look for young, firm,-fleshed vegetables and well-textured fish and meat.

should have a light marbling of fat. Fat not only enhances the flavour, but also guarantees that the meat will be moist and juicy to eat. Poultry should have pale meat that is slightly shiny.

With fish and seafood, the most important thing is freshness. Even if you are buying filleted fish, it is a good idea to look at the state of the whole fish before filleting, if possible. A sure sign of fresh fish is that the eyes are clear as glass and the gills are shining red. Eyes that are cloudy or have fallen in, and light grey or even brownish gills are signs that the fish is going off. Fish

and seafood should never have a 'fishy' smell. It is best to cook them on the day of purchase, but if you have to store them, wrap them loosely in greaseproof paper or foil and store in the refrigerator for no longer than one day.

The same rules are true for vegetables used in a stock fondue – only the best are good enough. Rather than greenhouse vegetables, choose ones grown out of doors organically, if possible. These will give you the genuine taste that the recipe should have. Baby vegetables, such as corn cobs and courgettes, are ideal.

Swiss cheese fondue

Economical

To achieve the right consistency, it is essential to use Gruyère and Emmental cheese. To be absolutely authentic, you should prepare the fondue using a Neuenburg white wine from the Wallis Canton, which can also be drunk during the meal. A glass of kirsch should not only be added to the fondue, but also served with it or after it as an aid to digestion.

Serves 4–6
1 large white loaf
400 g/14 oz Gruyère cheese
200 g/7 oz Emmental cheese
1 clove garlic
300 ml/¹/2 pint dry sparkling
   white wine
30 ml/2 tablespoons lemon juice
10 ml/2 teaspoons cornflour
30 ml/2 tablespoons kirsch
freshly grated nutmeg
freshly ground white pepper
To serve:
mixed pickles
gherkins
cocktail onions
Fruity fennel salad (see page 42)
Lamb's lettuce with mushrooms
   (see page 46)

**For 6 persons
approximately per portion:**
3,010 kJ/720 kcal
38 g protein, 32 g fat
62 g carbohydrate

● Approximate preparation
   time: 30 minutes

1. Cut the bread into bite-size pieces and put them on a plate.

2. Coarsely grate the cheese. Peel the garlic and cut it in half. Carefully rub a ceramic fondue pan with the cut surfaces of the garlic.

3. Put the white wine and lemon juice into the pan and bring to the boil over a medium heat.

4. Add the cheese, a little at a time, stirring constantly in figure-of-eight movements with a wooden spoon. Do not add more cheese until each addition has melted completely. Continue adding the cheese in this way until all the cheese is used up.

5. Stir together the cornflour and kirsch. Stir the cornflour paste into the cheese fondue and bring to the boil. Season to taste with nutmeg and pepper.

6. Transfer the fondue pan to the stand. During the meal it should keep bubbling gently. Spear the bread cubes with fondue forks and dip them into the cheese fondue. Then remove, twisting them slightly as you do.

7. Serve with mixed pickles, gherkins, cocktail onions, Fruity fennel salad and Lamb's lettuce with mushrooms.

Tip

You can adapt the cheese fondue at will. You could add 5–10 ml/1–2 teaspoons herbes de Provence, a pinch of cayenne pepper or 5–10 ml/1–2 teaspoons medium mustard. Garlic-lovers can add 3–4 cloves finely chopped garlic stirred into the cheese fondue. If necessary, you can use a stainless steel saucepan.

For this Swiss national dish you need genuine Swiss cheese. Serve with white wine, preferably from Switzerland.

Fondue bourguignonne

Easy

Pronounced 'fon-dew boor-guin-yon' this is the best-known meat fondue. Basically, it means frying diced beef fillet cubes in hot oil. Allow 150–200 g/5–7 oz meat per person. This fondue would probably not be so popular were it not for a whole range of sauces, dips and chutneys to serve with it. You will quickly discover whether you prefer the meat to be rare, medium or well cooked and can adjust the length of time it cooks in the hot oil. Now comes the best part: trying out the sauces. Mix ready-made sauces into new creations on your plate. Others will probably imitate you with enthusiasm.

Serves 4
For the sauce:
250 ml/8 fl oz mayonnaise
75–90 ml/5–6 tablespoons tomato
  ketchup
30 ml/2 tablespoons milk or
  single cream
15–30 ml/1–2 tablespoons brandy
pinch of sugar
dash of Worcestershire sauce
salt and freshly ground white pepper
For the fondue:
600–800 g/1¼–1¾ lb beef fillet
¾ litre/1¼ pints oil
salt and freshly ground white pepper
To serve:
salad
crusty white bread

> **Approximately per portion, using 800 g/1¾ lb beef fillet:**
> 2,845 kJ/680 kcal
> 39 g protein, 54 g fat
> 10 g carbohydrate
>
> ● Approximate preparation
>   time: 25 minutes

1. First make the sauce. Mix together the mayonnaise, tomato ketchup and milk or cream until thoroughly combined. Stir in the brandy and season to taste with salt, pepper, sugar and Worcestershire sauce.

2. Using a sharp knife, cut the beef fillet into cubes about 4 cm/ ¾ inch.

3. Heat the oil in a saucepan over a medium heat and then pour it into a fondue pan. Put this on the stand and adjust the burner. so that the oil remains hot, but does not overheat.

4. Spear each cube of meat with a fondue fork and hold it in the hot oil. Fry according to taste. Push the cube off the fork on to a plate, using a table fork. Season with salt and pepper or dip into the sauce.

5. Serve with salad, crusty white bread and red wine.

> ## Tip
>
> You can also use other meat, such as loin of beef, lamb or pork fillet, chicken breast fillet or turkey steaks.

Fondue bourguignonne – the original form of the oil fondue – tastes best with a good variety of sauces, salad and bread.

Fondue chinoise

Rather time-consuming

For a Chinese fondue, the cooking is done in stock instead of in oil. Take your time to prepare the ingredients well, because they all have to be finely sliced and decoratively arranged. Unlike a fondue bourguignonne, a Chinese fondue is served with hardly any sauces. Soy, oyster, hoisin or plum sauces may be used very sparingly as seasoning.

Serves 4
For the chicken stock:
1 bunch mixed fresh herbs
2 onions
1 bay leaf
2 cloves
5 ml/1 teaspoon peppercorns
1.75 kg/4–4¹/₂ lb chicken
2.5 litres/4¹/₄ pints water
salt
For the fondue:
200 g/7 oz beef fillet
300 g/11 oz chicken breast fillet
25 g/1 oz dried Chinese mushrooms
200 g/7 oz spinach
1 bunch spring onions
250 g/9 oz carrots
1 small head Chinese leaves
150 g/5 oz cellophane noodles
250 g/9 oz plaice fillets
4 raw prawns
120 ml/4 fl oz soy sauce
4 egg yolks
rice, to serve

Approximately per portion:
1,385 kJ/330 kcal
50 g protein, 13 g fat
6 g carbohydrate

● Approximate preparation
time: 3¹/₄ hours

1. First make the stock. Finely chop the herbs. Put the herbs, onions, bay leaf, cloves, peppercorns and chicken into a large saucepan. Add the water and bring to the boil over a medium heat. Cook, uncovered, for about 2¹/₂–3 hours, skimming off the scum from time to time.

2. Meanwhile, place the beef fillet and chicken breast fillets in the freezer for 2–3 hours.

3. Strain the stock and season with a little salt. Reserve the cooked chicken and use it for another recipe. Discard the flavourings in the strainer.

4. Put the dried Chinese mushrooms in a small bowl and cover with lukewarm water.

5. Separate the spinach leaves. Thinly slice the spring onions and carrots diagonally. Cut the thick ribs from the Chinese leaves and cut the leaves into thin strips.

6. Put the cellophane noodles in a bowl and cover with boiling water. Set aside to soak for about 10–15 minutes.

7. With a sharp knife, cut the plaice fillets into thin strips. Peel and devein the prawns.

8. Remove the meat from the freezer and cut into wafer-thin slices with a sharp knife.

9. Drain the noodles and the mushrooms. Arrange them decoratively, together with the spinach, spring onions, carrots, Chinese leaves, beef, chicken and fish, on large serving dishes.

10. Bring the stock to the boil in a large pan over a medium heat and place this on the stand.

11. Spoon the soy sauce into four small bowls and add 1 egg yolk to each bowl.

12. Put the prepared ingredients into the fondue scoops in portions and cook them in the stock. Dip the cooked ingredients in the soy and egg yolk sauce using a fork or chopsticks.

13. Serve with rice, China tea or white wine.

The lightest fondue among the classics is the Fondue chinoise. When you have finished eating the fondue the stock tastes even better, so you can serve it as soup.

Sausage fondue with olive mayonnaise

Economical • Quick

Serves 4–6
120 ml/4 fl oz mayonnaise
150 ml/¹/₄ pint yogurt
200 g/7 oz pimiento-stuffed
   green olives
1 onion
2 cloves garlic
1 bunch parsley
200 g/7 oz small bratwurst
   sausages, blanched
2 Krakowska sausages,
   about 300 g/11 oz
1 large pork sausage,
   about 250 g/9 oz
4 pork chipolatas or small grilling
   sausages, about 300 g/11 oz
³/₄ litre/1¹/₄ pints oil
salt and freshly ground white pepper
To serve:
mixed pickles
chilli sauce
mustard
Cucumber and garlic cheese
   (see page 38)
Pepper relish (see page 40)
Crispy salad with grains (see page 46)
crusty bread

**For 6 persons,
approximately per portion:**
3,295 kJ/785 kcal
22 g protein, 64 g fat
4 g carbohydrate

● Approximate preparation
   time: 30 minutes

---

1. Mix together the mayonnaise and the yogurt. Finely dice the olives and onion. Add them to the mayonnaise. Crush the garlic and stir it into the mayonnaise. Season to taste. Chop the parsley, and stir it into the mayonnaise.

2. Cut the sausages into 2 cm/³/₄ inch long pieces and arrange them on a plate.

3. Heat the oil in a saucepan over a medium heat, then pour it into a fondue pan. Transfer to the stand.

4. Spear the sausages on fondue forks and fry until cooked and golden brown. Transfer to a plate, then dip in the olive mayonnaise.

5. Serve with mixed pickles, gherkins, chilli sauce, mustard, Cucumber and garlic cheese, Pepper relish, Crispy salad with grains, bread and beer.

Cheese fondue with broccoli and croûtons

Economical

Serves 4–6
1 kg/2¹/₄ lb broccoli
750 g/1 lb 10 oz Granary bread
400 g/14 oz Appenzeller cheese
300 ml/¹/₂ pint dry cider
30 ml/2 tablespoons lemon juice
200 g/7 oz medium mature
   Gouda cheese
10 ml/2 teaspoons cornflour
30 ml/2 tablespoons water
freshly grated nutmeg
salt and freshly ground white pepper
To serve:
mixed pickles
gherkins
pickled chillies

**For 6 persons,
approximately per portion:**
2,985 kJ/715 kcal
41 g protein, 32 g fat
62 g carbohydrate

● Approximate preparation
   time: 50 minutes

---

1. Divide the broccoli into florets. Blanch them in boiling, salted water for 2–3 minutes. Drain, rinse in cold water and drain again.

2. Cut the bread into slices, cut off the crusts and toast it. Then cut the toast into cubes. Arrange the croûtons and broccoli on individual serving plates.

3. Put the cider and lemon juice in a ceramic fondue pan and bring to the boil. Coarsely grate the cheese and add it, a little at a time, stirring constantly in figure-of-eight movements until it has melted.

4. Mix together the cornflour and water to a smooth paste and stir it into the cheese fondue. Bring the fondue to the boil and season to taste with nutmeg and pepper.

5. Transfer the cheese fondue to the stand. Spear the croûtons and broccoli florets on fondue forks and dip them in the cheese .

6. Serve with mixed pickles, gherkins, pickled chillies and beer or dry cider.

Above: Cheese fondue with broccoli and croûtons
Below: Sausage fondue with olive mayonnaise

Smoked loin of pork and turkey fondue

Easy

Serves 4
300 ml/1/2 pint natural yogurt
45 ml/3 tablespoons mayonnaise
45–60 ml/3–4 tablespoons milk
1 onion
1 tablespoon bottled green
*   peppercorns*
1 bunch parsley
400 g/14 oz boneless smoked
*   loin of pork*
400 g/14 oz boneless smoked
*   turkey breast*
1 litre/1 3/4 pints light chicken stock
105 ml/7 tablespoons beer
*   (optional)*
6–8 bay leaves
10 juniper berries
salt

> **Approximately per portion:**
> 2,200 kJ/525 kcal
> 48 g protein, 35 g fat
> 5 g carbohydrate
>
> ● Approximate preparation
>   time: 45 minutes

1. Mix together the yogurt, mayonnaise and milk. Finely dice the onion. Finely chop the peppercorns. Stir the onion and peppercorns into the yogurt mayonnaise and season with salt.

2. Reserve a few sprigs of parsley to garnish and finely chop the remaining leaves. Stir the chopped parsley into the yogurt mayonnaise and set aside.

3. Dice the pork and turkey breast into bite-size pieces and arrange them on a plate.

4. Put the chicken stock, the beer if using, the bay leaves and the juniper berries into a saucepan and bring to the boil. Pour the mixture into a fondue pan and transfer it to the stand.

5. Spear the meat cubes on fondue forks and heat them in the stock. Serve with the yogurt mayonnaise.

Tip

This recipe tastes good with tomato ketchup, Roquefort cream (see page 36), Cucumber and garlic cheese (see page 38), Crispy salad with grains (see page 46), caraway bread, Granary bread and beer.

Meat loaf fondue with mooli salad

Easy

Serves 4
1 large mooli
15 ml/1 tablespoon sunflower seeds
800 g/1 3/4 lb meat loaf
15 ml/1 tablespoon white
*   wine vinegar*
pinch of sugar
45 ml/3 tablespoons soya oil
1 bunch parsley
750 ml /1 1/4 pints oil
salt and freshly ground
*   white pepper*

> **Approximately per portion:**
> 3,730 kJ/890 kcal
> 25 g protein, 87 g fat
> 1 g carbohydrate
>
> ● Approximate preparation
>   time: 45 minutes

1. Peel the mooli and cut it into thin slices. Sprinkle with a little salt and set aside for about 15 minutes.

2. Dry-fry the sunflower seeds in a frying pan. Tip them on to a plate and set aside to cool. Cut the meat loaf into bite-size pieces.

3. Mix the vinegar in a bowl with the sugar and salt and pepper to taste. Gradually stir in the oil. Gently squeeze the water from the mooli and mix it with the marinade. Chop the parsley, mix it into the mooli, transfer to a salad bowl and sprinkle over the sunflower seeds.

4. Heat the oil in a saucepan, pour it into a fondue pan and transfer to the stand. Spear the meat loaf on fondue forks and fry in the oil until crisp. Serve with the mooli salad.

Tip

This fondue is delicious served with creamed horseradish, Tomato chutney (see page 40), mustard, pretzels or bread rolls and beer.

Above: Meat loaf fondue with mooli salad
Below: Smoked loin of pork and turkey fondue

Cheese and ham fondue

Economical • Easy to make

1 kg/2¼ lb small firm potatoes
30 ml/2 tablespoons caraway seeds
50 g/2 oz raw ham
5 ml/1 teaspoon vegetable oil
450g/1 lb Emmental cheese
300 ml/½ pint white wine
10 ml/2 teaspoons lemon juice
150 g/5 oz full-fat cream cheese
   with herbs
10 ml/2 teaspoons cornflour
30 ml/2 tablespoons water
freshly ground nutmeg
freshly ground white pepper

Approximately per portion:
3,255 kJ/780 kcal
44 g protein, 48 g fat
38 g carbohydrate

● Approximate preparation
   time: 1 hour

1. Wash the potatoes, but do not peel them. Put them in a saucepan, together with the caraway seeds, and add sufficient water just to cover. Bring to the boil, cover and cook over a medium heat for 20–25 minutes, or until they are tender.

2. Finely dice the ham. Heat the oil in a saucepan, add the ham and fry, stirring frequently, until crisp. Coarsely grate the Emmental cheese. Put the ham, white wine and lemon juice in a ceramic fondue pan and bring to the boil.

3. Gradually add the grated cheese to the wine, stirring constantly, in figure-of-eight movements with a wooden spoon until the cheese has melted. Mix in the cream cheese a little at a time. Mix together the cornflour and water to a smooth paste and stir it in. Bring to the boil and season to taste with nutmeg and pepper.

4. Serve the potatoes with or without their skins, as desired. At the table, cut the potatoes in half or quarters and dip them into the cheese and ham fondue.

Tip

Serve this fondue with Pepper salad with sprouted seeds (see page 44), mixed pickles, gherkins and beer or rosé wine.

Fondue with meatballs

Economical

Serves 4
1 1/2 bread rolls
2 onions
750 g/1 lb 10 oz mixed minced
   meat
30 ml/2 tablespoons medium
   mustard
1 large egg
10 ml/2 teaspoons dried marjoram
breadcrumbs (optional)
115 g/4 oz ewe's milk cheese
20–25 pimiento-stuffed olives
750 ml/1 1/4 pints vegetable oil
salt and freshly ground white pepper
parsley sprigs, to garnish

Approximately per portion:
3,020 kJ/720 kcal
55 g protein, 52 g fat
8 g carbohydrate

● Approximate preparation
  time: 1 hour

Tip

For each 500 g/1 1/4 lb minced
meat, allow about 7.5 ml/1 1/2
teaspoons salt and
1.5–2.5/1/4–1/2 teaspoon
pepper. The meatballs can also
be shaped into kebabs. Serve
with Curry sauce (see page 36),
Cranberry and onion sauce
(see page 38), cucumber and
carrot salad, Crispy salad with
seeds (see page 46), lager or
white wine spritzer.

1. Put the rolls in a shallow dish, pour over a little lukewarm water and set aside to soften. Finely dice the onions. Put the minced meat into a large bowl, together with the onions, mustard, egg and marjoram and season to taste with salt and pepper.

2. Squeeze the excess water out of the bread rolls and add them to the mixture. Knead the mixture using the dough hooks of an electric mixer until smooth. If the mixture is too soft, add some breadcrumbs, mixing well.

3. Dice the cheese into 1 cm/ 1/2 inch cubes. Form the minced meat mixture into balls by rolling portions between the palms of your hands. Stuff half the meatballs with 1 olive each and the other half with 1 cheese cube each.

4. Arrange the meatballs side by side on serving plates and garnish with parsley sprigs. Heat the oil in a saucepan, pour it into a fondue pan and transfer to the stand. Spear the meatballs with fondue forks and fry them in the oil until brown and crisp.

Fish fondue with dill

Rather time-consuming

Serves 4
250 g/9 oz spinach
400 g/14 oz sole or plaice fillets
400 g/14 oz salmon trout fillet
200 ml/7 fl oz double cream
150 ml/¹/₄ pint soured cream or
*   natural yogurt*
pinch of ground coriander
dash of lemon juice
1 orange
60 ml/4 tablespoons mayonnaise
pinch of cayenne pepper
5–10 ml/1–2 teaspoons clear honey
1 litre/1³/₄ pints light chicken stock
2 bunches dill
salt and freshly ground white pepper
To serve:
green salad
vinaigrette dressing
crusty white bread

Approximately per portion:
2,435 kJ/580 kcal
42 g protein, 43 g fat
6 g carbohydrate

● Approximate preparation
time: 1 hour

1. Trim the stalks from the spinach. Blanch the leaves in a large saucepan of boiling, salted water for about 1 minute. Drain and squeeze out as much moisture as possible.

2. Cut the fish into bite-size cubes. Arrange the salmon trout cubes on serving plates or dishes.

3. Lay 2–3 large spinach leaves on top of each other so that the edges overlap. Put a cube of sole or plaice on top and wrap the leaves securely around it. Continue making spinach parcels in this way until all the sole or plaice has been used up. Transfer the parcels to the serving plates or dishes.

4. Finely chop the remaining spinach. Beat the double cream until it is thick, but not stiff. Mix half the beaten cream with the chopped spinach and the soured cream or yogurt. Season to taste with ground coriander, lemon juice, salt and pepper.

5. Finely grate the orange rind and squeeze out the juice. Mix together the orange rind, orange juice and mayonnaise. Stir in the remaining double cream and season to taste with cayenne pepper and salt. Stir in the honey and transfer to a small bowl.

6. Heat the stock in a large saucepan over a medium heat and transfer it to a stand. Add the dill to the stock and adjust the burner so that it is gently bubbling. Spear the fish on fondue forks and cook it in the stock.

7. Serve with green salad tossed in a vinaigrette dressing, crusty white bread and dry white wine.

Tip

You can also use blanched Chinese leaves or young cabbage leaves to wrap around the sole or plaice fillets. Spear the parcels right through, so that the leaves do not unwrap.

This fine fondue also tastes wonderful with stock flavoured with dill flowers. Unfortunately, they are available for only a short time during the year and are difficult to obtain. As well as the sauces named, it also goes well with crème fraîche mixed with all kinds of fresh herbs.

Fondue with marinated meat

Exquisite • Low calorie

Serves 4
600 g/1 lb 5 oz beef, pork or lamb
*   fillet (mixed if possible)*
3 cloves garlic
6 juniper berries
1 lemon
6–8 sprigs fresh mint or lemon balm
1 litre/1³/4 pints light chicken stock
freshly ground black pepper
lettuce leaves, to garnish
To serve:
Avocado dip (see page 36)
Roquefort cream (see page 36)
Salad with asparagus and rocket (see
*   page 42)*
baguette

Approximately per portion:
920 kJ/220 kcal
30 g protein, 11 g fat
1 g carbohydrate

● Approximate preparation
time: 2¹/2 hours of which
2 hours are marinating time

---

1. With a sharp knife, cut the meat into thin slices.

2. Finely dice the garlic. Pound the juniper berries in a mortar with a pestle. Grate the lemon rind. Chop the mint or lemon balm leaves. Mix together the garlic, juniper berries, lemon rind and mint or lemon balm and season to taste with pepper.

3. Rub the marinade all over the slices of meat. Lay the slices on top of one another and wrap them in

clear film. Set aside in the refrigerator to marinate for about 2 hours.

4. Arrange the meat on a bed of lettuce leaves.

5. Heat the stock in a saucepan, then pour it into a fondue pan and transfer it to the stand.

6. Spear the meat slices with fondue forks and cook them in the gently bubbling stock.

7. Serve with Avocado dip and Roquefort cream, Salad with asparagus and rocket, a fresh baguette and red or white wine.

Seafood fondue

Rather expensive

Serves 4
1 onion
15 ml/1 tablespoon olive oil
120 ml/4 fl oz dry white wine or
*   chicken stock*
30 ml/2 tablespoons pernod
1 kg/2¹/4 lb mussels, scrubbed and
*   debearded*
400 g/14 oz raw prawns
750 ml/1¹/4 pints vegetable oil
250 ml/8 fl oz crème fraîche
1 bunch dill
salt and freshly ground white pepper
crusty white bread, to serve

Approximately per portion:
1,845 kJ/440 kcal
30 g protein, 42 g fat
4 g carbohydrate

● Approximate preparation
time: 45 minutes

---

1. Dice the onion. Heat the olive oil in a large saucepan. Add the onion and sauté until it is soft and translucent. Add the white wine or chicken stock and pernod. Add the mussels, cover and cook over a high heat, shaking the pan from time to time, for about 5 minutes.

2. Peel and devein the prawns. Drain the mussels, reserving the cooking liquid. Remove the mussels from their shells. Discard any mussels that remain closed. Arrange the mussels and prawns on a serving plate.

3. Mix the crème fraîche with 45–60 ml/3–4 tablespoons of the reserved cooking liquid. Season to taste with salt and pepper. Finely chop the dill and stir it into the crème fraîche mixture.

4. Heat the oil in a saucepan, pour it into a fondue pan and transfer it to the stand.

5. Spear the mussels and prawns on fondue forks and fry them in the hot oil. Serve with the crème fraîche sauce, crusty white bread and dry white wine.

Tip

This fondue also goes well with Crème fraîche with tomato (see page 34) and Mustard mayonnaise with dill (see page 38).

Above: Fondue with marinated meat
Below: Seafood fondue

Japanese fondue Shabushabu

Exquisite • Rather time-consuming

Serves 4
400 g/14 oz beef fillet
20 g/³/4 oz dried shiitake
   mushrooms
250 g/9 oz Chinese leaves
200 g/7 oz cellophane noodles
200 g/7 oz mushrooms
150 g/5 oz mooli
200 g/7 oz spinach
105 ml/7 tablespoons lemon juice
45 ml/3 tablespoons soy sauce
45 ml/3 tablespoons water
2 spring onions
60 ml/4 tablespoons sesame seeds
15 ml/1 tablespoon sugar
15 ml/1 tablespoon miso
   (soya bean paste)
30 ml/2 tablespoons sweet rice wine
   or sweet sherry
15 ml/1 tablespoon fruit vinegar
5 ml/1 teaspoon mustard powder
1.5 litres/2¹/2 pints light
   chicken stock

Approximately per portion:
1,295 kJ/310 kcal
30 g protein, 13 g fat
10 g carbohydrate

● Approximate preparation
  time: 2¹/2–3¹/2 hours of which
  2–3 hours are freezing time

Tip

This recipe goes well with rice,
dry white wine, mineral water
or green tea.

1. Put the beef fillet in the freezer for 2–3 hours. Put the shiitake mushrooms in a small bowl, cover with boiling water and set aside to soak for about 30 minutes.

2. Remove the stems from the Chinese leaves and shred the leaves. Put the cellophane noodles in a bowl, cover with boiling water and set aside to soak for 5 minutes. Slice the mushrooms. Peel the mooli and cut 115 g/4 oz of it into matchsticks.

3. Drain the noodles and cut them up with kitchen scissors. Drain the shiitake mushrooms. Arrange the noodles, mushrooms, shiitake mushrooms, Chinese leaves, mooli matchsticks and spinach decoratively on a serving plate.

4. Mix together the lemon juice, soy sauce and water and pour it into a bowl.

5. Finely grate the remaining mooli. Thinly slice the spring onions into rings. Put them into separate bowls.

6. Dry-fry the sesame seeds in a frying pan over a medium heat. Pound them in the mortar with a pestle. Mix together the sugar, miso, rice wine, vinegar, mustard powder and sesame seeds in a small serving bowl.

7. Cut the meat into wafer-thin slices with a sharp knife. Arrange the slices on a serving plate.

8. Heat the stock in a flat wide saucepan and transfer it to a stand. Everyone at the table collects the prepared ingredients in a scoop and holds this in the stock to cook them. They are eaten together with the two sauces, the spring onions and the grated mooli.

Tip

Shabu means shake in Japanese. This makes sense when we remember that the Japanese eat with chopsticks. They pick up the slices of meat with the chopsticks, swing it twice through the stock – shabushabu – and the meat is cooked. You could try it sometime. The technique is easily mastered with a little practice. Hold one chopstick firmly in the bend between thumb and index finger and rest it on your middle finger. The second chopstick does the guiding, held by the thumb and index finger. Wooden chopsticks are best because the meat slices do not fall off so easily as they do from lacquered chopsticks.

Mushroom fondue with poultry

Exquisite • Easy

Serves 4
10 dried ceps
120 ml/4 fl oz lukewarm water
1 bunch parsley
1 sprig rosemary
2 sprigs thyme
2 bay leaves
1.5 litres/2¹/2 pints light
   chicken stock
2 bunches spring onions
400 g/14 oz turkey steaks
300 g/11 oz skinless, boneless
   chicken breasts
750 g/1 lb 10 oz button mushrooms
10 ml/2 teaspoons bottled green
   peppercorns
200 ml/7 fl oz crème fraîche
salt and freshly ground
   black pepper
fresh bay leaves, to
   garnish (optional)
To serve:
Crème fraîche with tomato
   (see page 34)
Roquefort cream (see page 36)
Endive salad with red lentils
   (see page 44)
crusty bread

Approximately per portion:
1,840 kJ/440 kcal
49 g protein, 23 g fat
5 g carbohydrate

● Approximate preparation
  time: 50 minutes

---

1. Finely chop the ceps and put them in a small bowl. Cover with the lukewarm water and set aside to soak.

2. Pull the parsley leaves off their stalks. Tie the parsley stalks, together with the rosemary, thyme and bay leaves, into a bundle.

3. Put the stock, the ceps, together with their soaking water, and the herb bundle into a saucepan. Bring to a boil, then simmer over a low heat for about 30 minutes.

4. Meanwhile, cut the spring onions into 4 cm/1¹/2 inch long pieces. Cut the turkey steaks and chicken breasts into thin strips. Arrange the spring onions, button mushrooms, turkey and chicken on serving plates and garnish with bay leaves, if using.

5. Chop the parsley leaves and the green peppercorns. Stir them into the crème fraîche and season to taste with salt and pepper.

6. Remove the herb bundle from the stock and discard. Pour the stock into a fondue pan and transfer it to a stand. Adjust the burner so that the stock is just gently bubbling.

7. Spear the vegetables and meat on fondue forks and cook them in the stock. Serve with the seasoned crème fraîche and Crème fraîche with tomato, Roquefort cream, Endive salad with red lentils, crusty bread and a light rosé wine.

Tip

Dried ceps, also known as porcini, give an intense mushroom flavour not only to stocks but also to soups, stews and sauces. It is important to rinse the mushrooms because they are sometimes quite sandy. Before using them, soak them in lukewarm water. You should always use the soaking water in the cooking.

As well as crème fraîche seasoned with green peppercorns (top), this light mushroom fondue goes well with Crème fraîche with tomato (centre) and Roquefort cream (bottom).

Fondue with spring vegetables

Vegetarian • Low calorie

Serves 4
3 shallots
1 lime
150 ml/¼ pint natural yogurt
60 ml/4 tablespoons mayonnaise
pinch of sugar
½ bunch chervil or 1 bunch parsley
500 g/1¼ lb white asparagus
500 g/1¼ lb green asparagus
250 g/9 oz mangetout
500 g/1¼ lb young carrots
2 kohlrabi
1.5 litres/1¾ pints light
   vegetable stock
salt and freshly ground
   white pepper

Approximately per portion:
960 kJ/230 kcal
12 g protein, 15 g fat
17 g carbohydrate

● Approximate preparation
   time: 1 hour

Tip

Use only fresh chervil, as it does not dry well. It goes well with egg dishes, vegetables, poultry and fish.
This dish can also be served with Mustard mayonnaise with dill (see page 38), herb-flavoured soft cheese, French bread and dry white wine or mineral water.

1. Dice the shallots. Grate the lime rind and squeeze the juice. Mix together the shallots, lime rind, lime juice, yogurt and mayonnaise. Season to taste with salt and pepper and stir in the sugar. Chop the chervil or parsley and stir it into the mixture.

2. Peel the white asparagus, cut off the woody ends of the stems and slice diagonally into thin pieces. Trim the woody ends of the green asparagus and slice the stems diagonally into thin pieces.

3. Trim the mangetout. Slice the carrots diagonally. Thinly slice the kohlrabi. Arrange all the vegetables decoratively on a serving plate.

4. Heat the stock in a large saucepan and transfer it to a stand. Put a few vegetables at a time into fondue scoops and cook them in the stock. Serve with the chervil or parsley sauce.

Tofu fondue in soy stock

Low calorie • Rather time-consuming

Serves 4
*600 g/1 lb 5 oz tofu
40 g/1 1/2 oz fresh root ginger
120 ml/4 fl oz medium dry sherry
30 ml/2 tablespoons soya oil
5 ml/1 teaspoon crushed
   dried chilli
1 mooli
1 head Chinese leaves
1.5 litres/2 1/2 pints light
   chicken stock
45–60 ml/3–4 tablespoons light
   soy sauce
freshly ground white pepper*

Approximately per portion:
1,025 kJ/245 kcal
13 g protein, 12 g fat
9 g carbohydrate

● Approximate preparation
   time: 4 1/2 hours of which
   4 hours are marinating time

Tip

This fondue is delicious with soy
sauce, chilli sauce, rice, Pepper
relish (see page 40) and dry
white wine.

1. Dice the tofu into small cubes
and put them into a shallow bowl.

2. Peel and finely grate the root
ginger. Mix together the sherry, oil,
chilli and ginger and season with
pepper. Pour over the diced tofu
and mix thoroughly. Set aside to
marinate for 4 hours.

3. Peel the mooli and cut the flesh
into matchstick strips. Cut the thick
stems from the Chinese leaves and
shred the leaves. Arrange the
mooli and Chinese leaves on a
serving plate.

4. Put the chicken stock, soy sauce
and 60 ml/4 tablespoons of the
marinade in a large saucepan, heat
well and transfer to a stand. Put
the tofu cubes with the mooli and
Chinese leaves into fondue scoops
and cook them in the stock.

Fish fondue

Easy • Quick

Serves 4
500 g/1¼ lb fish trimmings, such
*   as bones, skin and heads*
2 onions
1 bay leaf
6 juniper berries
1 bunch dill
1 bunch parsley
1.5 litres/2½ pints water
120 ml/4 fl oz dry white wine
400 g/14 oz haddock fillet
400 g/14 oz pollack fillet
300 ml/½ pint natural yogurt
30 ml/2 tablespoons double cream
5–10 ml/1–2 teaspoons grated
*   fresh horseradish or*
*   creamed horseradish*
dash of lemon juice
salt and freshly ground white pepper
To garnish:
lemon wedges
dill sprigs

Approximately per portion:
1,135 kJ/270 kcal
39 g protein, 9 g fat
4 g carbohydrate

● Approximate preparation
  time: 40 minutes

---

1. Put the fish trimmings into a saucepan. Peel and quarter the onions and add them to the saucepan, together with the bay leaf and the juniper berries. Cut off the herb stalks and add them to the saucepan. Reserve the leaves.

2. Add the water and the wine and bring to the boil over a medium heat. Simmer, uncovered, over a low heat for about 20 minutes.

3. Rinse the fish fillets and dice into bite-size cubes. Arrange them on serving plates and garnish with lemon wedges and dill sprigs.

4. Finely chop the reserved herb leaves. Mix them with the yogurt and cream, season to taste with salt and pepper and stir in the horseradish and lemon juice.

5. Strain the fish stock into a large saucepan and season to taste with salt and pepper. Transfer the saucepan to a stand.

6. Spear the fish cubes on fondue forks and cook them in the stock. Then dip them into the horseradish and yogurt sauce.

Poultry fondue with nut dip

Easy

Serves 4
25 g/1 oz shelled pistachio nuts
40 g/1½ oz shelled almonds
105 ml/7 tablespoons double cream
150 ml/¼ pint crème fraîche
pinch of cayenne pepper
300 g/11 oz chicken breast fillets
300 g/11 oz turkey breast fillets
1 duck breast fillet
1 pointed cabbage or 1 head
*   Chinese leaves*
1.5 litres/2½ pints light
*   chicken stock*
salt
parsley sprigs, to garnish
cherry tomatoes, to serve

Approximately per portion:
2,370 kJ/565 kcal
46 g protein, 37 g fat
13 g carbohydrate

● Approximate preparation
  time: 50 minutes

---

1. Finely chop the pistachio nuts. Finely grind the almonds. Beat the double cream until it is thick, but not stiff. Mix the cream with the crème fraîche and add the nuts. Season to taste with salt and cayenne pepper.

2. Thinly slice the chicken and turkey. Remove the skin from the duck breast and cut the flesh into thin slices. Arrange the meat on serving plates. and garnish with parsley sprigs.

3. Shred the cabbage or Chinese leaves and put them on a serving plate.

4. Heat the chicken stock in a large saucepan and transfer it to a stand. Put the meat slices and the cabbage into fondue scoops and cook them in the stock. Serve with the nut dip and cherry tomatoes.

Tip

This dish can also be served with Avocado dip (see page 36) and Redcurrant and pear chutney (see page 40).

Above: Fish fondue
Below: Poultry fondue with nut dip

Egg and gherkin smetana

Economical • Easy

Smetana is a soured cream with low fat content. You will be able to find it in the chill cabinet in most supermarkets. Otherwise you can use crème fraîche.

Serves 4
1–2 eggs
1 onion
2 gherkins (about 115 g/4 oz)
250 ml/8 fl oz smetana
105 ml/7 tablespoons double cream
1 bunch parsley
salt and freshly ground white pepper
finely chopped hard-boiled egg and
parsley, to garnish

Approximately per portion:
1,420 kJ/340 kcal
6 g protein, 34 g fat
4 g carbohydrate

● Approximate preparation time: 15 minutes

1. Cook the eggs in boiling water for 10 minutes.

2. Dice the onion and gherkins into small cubes. Mix together the smetana and double cream and stir in the gherkins. Season to taste with salt and pepper.

3. Chop the parsley. Rinse the eggs in cold water, shell and dice them. Stir them into the smetana, together with the parsley, and season again, if necessary. Garnish with chopped egg and parsley.

Crème fraîche with tomato

Easy

Serves 4
250 g/9 oz tomatoes
1 onion
2 spring onions
250 ml/8 fl oz crème fraîche
15 ml/1 tablespoon tomato ketchup
salt and freshly ground white pepper
diced tomato and thinly sliced spring
onion, to garnish

Approximately per portion:
1,070 kJ/255 kcal
2 g protein, 25 g fat
5 g carbohydrate

● Approximate preparation time: 30 minutes

1. Cut a wedge out of the tomatoes where the stalk is attached and cut a cross on the opposite side. Put them in a bowl, pour boiling water over them and set aside for 5 minutes.

2. Finely dice the onion. Thinly slice the spring onions into rings.

3. Rinse the tomatoes in cold water and peel. Seed and then dice the flesh.

4. Mix together the crème fraîche, tomatoes, onion and spring onions and season well with salt and pepper. Garnish with diced tomato and sliced spring onion.

Anchovy yogurt sauce

Economical • Easy

Serves 4
300 ml/1/2 pint natural yogurt
5 ml/1 teaspoon olive oil
2 cloves garlic
50 g/2 oz canned anchovy
fillets, drained
1 bunch chives
salt and freshly ground white pepper
anchovy fillets and snipped chives,
to garnish

Approximately per portion:
370 kJ/ 90 kcal
5 g protein, 6 g fat
4 g carbohydrate

● Approximate preparation time: 15 minutes

1. Mix together the yogurt and olive oil. Crush the garlic and stir it into the mixture.

2. Rinse the anchovies in cold water, pat dry with absorbent kitchen paper and remove any bones with tweezers. Finely chop the anchovy fillets.

3. Snip the chives into thin rings. Stir them into the yogurt, together with the anchovies. Season with salt and pepper and garnish with anchovy fillets and snipped chives.

Above: Egg and gherkin smetana
Centre: Crème fraîche with tomato
Below: Anchovy yogurt sauce

Avocado dip

Easy • Quick

Serves 4
2 large ripe avocados
juice of 1 lime
3 shallots
105 ml/7 tablespoons soured cream
  or natural yogurt
1.5–2.5 ml/¹/4–¹/2 teaspoon crushed
  dried chilli
15 ml/1 tablespoon gin, (optional)
salt and freshly ground white pepper
diced avocado, to garnish

Approximately per portion:
1,055 kJ/250 kcal
3 g protein, 25 g fat
2 g carbohydrate

- Approximate preparation
  time: 25 minutes

---

1. Cut the avocados in half and remove the stones. Scoop out the flesh with a tablespoon and put it into a mixing bowl. Add the lime juice and beat with a hand-held mixer to make a smooth purée.

2. Finely dice the shallots and add them to the avocados, together with the soured cream or yogurt. Season to taste with salt, pepper and stir in the chilli and gin, if using. Garnish with diced avocado.

Tip

Prepare the avocado dip shortly before serving because it loses its colour if left standing.

Curry sauce

Exquisite • Easy

Curry powder is a mixture of at least 12 spices. It ranges from mild to very hot, so you should measure it carefully and add any other seasoning afterwards.

Serves 4
2 shallots
200 ml/7 fl oz mayonnaise
15–20 ml/3–4 teaspoons medium
  curry powder
90 ml/6 tablespoons mango chutney
150 ml/¹/4 pint soured cream
1 lime
pinch of cayenne pepper
6 sprigs fresh mint (optional)
salt

Approximately per portion:
1,375 kJ/330 kcal
2 g protein, 30 g fat
14 g carbohydrate

- Approximate preparation
  time: 15 minutes

---

1. Finely dice the shallots. Mix together the mayonnaise, curry powder, mango chutney, soured cream and shallots.

2. Finely grate the lime rind and squeeze the juice. Mix the rind and juice into the curry sauce. Season to taste with cayenne pepper and salt.

3. If using, cut the mint leaves into thin strips and stir into the sauce.

Roquefort cream

Easy

Serves 4
115 g/4 oz Roquefort cheese
115 g/4 oz full-fat cream cheese
200 ml/7 fl oz double cream
40 g/1¹/2 oz shelled walnuts
3 spring onions
salt and freshly ground white pepper
walnut halves, to garnish

Approximately per portion:
1,670 kJ/400 kcal
11 g protein, 37 g fat
4 g carbohydrate

- Approximate preparation
  time: 25 minutes

---

1. Put the Roquefort cheese and the cream cheese into a bowl and mash thoroughly with a fork. Gradually pour in the cream and beat the mixture until smooth.

2. Finely chop the walnuts. Finely chop the spring onions. Mix the walnuts and spring onions into the Roquefort cream. Season to taste with salt and pepper and garnish with walnut halves.

Above: Roquefort cream
Centre: Curry sauce
Below: Avocado dip

Mustard mayonnaise with dill

Exquisite • Easy

Serves 4–6
2 egg yolks
pinch of sugar
15 ml/1 tablespoon tarragon vinegar
20 ml/4 teaspoons strong mustard
10 ml/2 teaspoons wholegrain
  mustard
20 ml/4 teaspoons sweet,
  mild mustard
about 1/4 litre/8 fl oz oil
1 bunch dill
salt and freshly ground white pepper
dill sprig, to garnish

**For 6 persons,
approximately per portion:**
1,670 kJ/400 kcal
1 g protein, 44 g fat
0 g carbohydrate

● Approximate preparation
  time: 25 minutes

---

1. Put the egg yolks, sugar, vinegar and the three types of mustard into a mixing bowl and season to taste with salt and pepper. Beat with a hand-held electric mixer to form a smooth cream.

2. With the motor still running, add the oil, drop by drop, to form a smooth mayonnaise.

3. Finely chop the dill and stir it into the mayonnaise. Season the mustard mayonnaise with salt and pepper again just before serving, garnished with a dill sprig.

Cucumber and garlic cheese

Economical

Serves 4
150 g/5 oz cucumber
250 g/9 oz full-fat curd cheese
200 g/7 oz buttermilk
30 ml/2 tablespoons olive oil
1 onion
3 cloves garlic
50 g/2 oz black olives, stoned
1 bunch dill
salt and freshly ground black pepper
cucumber matchsticks, to garnish

Approximately per portion:
975 kJ/230 kcal
9 g protein, 18 g fat
7 g carbohydrate

● Approximate preparation
  time: 30 minutes

---

1. Cut the cucumber in half lengthways and scoop out the seeds with a teaspoon. Coarsely grate the flesh. Sprinkle it with a little salt and set aside for about 15 minutes.

2. Mix together the curd cheese, buttermilk and olive oil. Finely dice the onion and garlic and stir them into the cheese mixture. Finely dice the olives and stir them into the cheese mixture.

3. Drain the cucumber, squeezing out as much moisture as possible, and mix it into the cheese. Season to taste with salt and pepper. Finely chop the dill and stir it in. Garnish with cucumber matchsticks.

Cranberry and onion sauce

Easy • Quick

Serves 4
115 g/4 oz drained cocktail onions
225 g/8 oz canned cranberries
120 ml/4 fl oz mayonnaise
pinch of cayenne pepper
5 ml/1 teaspoon crushed dried chilli
salt

Approximately per portion:
910 kJ/220 kcal
0 g protein, 13 g fat
24 g carbohydrate

● Approximate preparation
  time: 10 minutes

---

1. Coarsely chop the cocktail onions.

2. Mix together the cocktail onions, cranberries and mayonnaise. Stir in the cayenne pepper and chilli and season to taste with salt.

Above: Mustard mayonnaise with dill
Centre: Cucumber and garlic cheese
Below: Cranberry and onion sauce

Redcurrant and pear chutney

Can be prepared in advance

Serves 4
2 pears, about 200 g/7 oz
375 g/12 oz redcurrants
2.5 cm/1 inch piece fresh root ginger
75 g/3 oz shallots
5 ml/1 teaspoon bottled green
    peppercorns
200 g/7 oz sugar
90 ml/6 tablespoons white
    wine vinegar
120 ml/4 fl oz water

Approximately per portion:
1,125 kJ/270 kcal
2 g protein, 1 g fat
40 g carbohydrate

● Approximate preparation
   time: 45 minutes

---

1. Quarter, core and finely chop the pears. Strip the redcurrants from their stalks with a fork.

2. Peel and finely grate the ginger. Dice the shallots.

3. Put the pears, redcurrants, ginger and shallots into a saucepan, together with the peppercorns, sugar, vinegar and water. Bring to the boil and simmer over a medium heat, stirring occasionally, for 10–15 minutes, until thickened. Transfer the chutney to a bowl and set aside to cool.

Tomato chutney

Can be prepared in advance

Serves 4
750 g/1 lb 10 oz tomatoes
250 g/9 oz onions
2 fresh red chillies
45 ml/3 tablespoons oil
6 cloves
150 ml/1 1/4 pint red wine vinegar
150 g/5 oz brown sugar
pinch of freshly grated nutmeg
salt and freshly ground
    white pepper

Approximately per portion:
885 kJ/210 kcal
3 g protein, 1 g fat
47 g carbohydrate

● Approximate preparation
   time: 1 hour

---

1. Make small cuts in the tomatoes, put them in a bowl and pour boiling water over them. Drain, rinse in cold water and peel. Seed and dice the flesh.

2. Dice the onions. Seed and dice the chillies.

3. Heat the oil in a large saucepan. Add the onions and sauté until soft and translucent. Add the tomatoes, chillies, cloves, vinegar, sugar and nutmeg and season to taste with salt and pepper. Bring to the boil and simmer over a medium heat, stirring occasionally, for about 20 minutes. Spoon the chutney into a bowl and set aside to cool.

Pepper relish

Economical

Serves 4
350 g/12 oz peppers
130 g/4 1/2 oz onions
30 ml/2 tablespoons vegetable oil
30 ml/2 tablespoons mustard seeds
120 ml/4 fl oz dry white wine
90 ml/6 tablespoons vinegar
30 ml/2 tablespoons salt
10 ml/2 teaspoons sugar
1 small cucumber
freshly ground white pepper

Approximately per portion:
480 kJ/115 kcal
2 g protein, 5 g fat
9 g carbohydrate

● Approximate preparation
   time: 50 minutes

---

1. Seed and dice the peppers. Dice the onions. Heat the oil in a saucepan. Add the onions and mustard seeds and sauté until the onions are soft. Add the peppers and sauté for 1–2 minutes.

2. Add the wine, vinegar and sugar and season to taste with salt and pepper. Bring to the boil and simmer over a medium heat for about 10 minutes.

3. Peel and seed the cucumber and finely dice the flesh. Stir it into the pepper relish and simmer for a further 10 minutes. Transfer to a bowl and set aside to cool.

Above: Redcurrant and pear chutney
Centre: Tomato chutney
Below: Pepper relish

Fruity fennel salad

Easy

Serves 4
4 fennel bulbs, about
  600 g/1 lb 5 oz
250 g/9 oz black grapes
4 oranges
juice of 1 lime or 1 lemon
1 tablespoon aniseed liqueur,
  ouzo or grape juice
2–3 drops Tabasco sauce
45 ml/3 tablespoons sunflower oil
4 sprigs lemon balm
15 ml/1 tablespoon pumpkin
  seeds
freshly ground white pepper
lemon balm sprigs, to garnish

Approximately per portion:
825 kJ/195 kcal
5 g protein, 9 g fat
25 g carbohydrate

● Approximate preparation
  time: 30 minutes

---

1. Cut the fennel into thin strips, reserving the green fronds for the garnish. Halve and seed the grapes. Using a sharp knife, peel the oranges, remove all the white pith and cut the flesh into segments, working over a bowl to catch the juice.

2. Mix together the lime juice, aniseed liqueur, ouzo or grape juice, Tabasco sauce and any reserved orange juice. Season to taste with pepper. Gradually beat in the oil. Add the fennel, grapes and orange segments and toss thoroughly to coat.

3. Cut the lemon balm leaves into strips and chop the fennel fronds. Sprinkle them over the salad, together with the pumpkin seeds. Garnish with lemon balm sprigs and serve.

Tip

The best way to prepare citrus fruits is, firstly, peel the fruit like an apple. Carefully cut away the white pitch. Then, with a sharp knife, cut along the membranes surrounding the individual segments and remove them.

Salad with asparagus and rocket

Exquisite • Easy

Rocket is also called roquette, rucola and arugula. It has a strong, sharp taste that is slightly peppery, so it is best mixed with other milder-tasting salad leaves.

Serves 4
4 small shallots
45 ml/3 tablespoons tarragon
  vinegar
5 ml/1 teaspoon medium mustard
1 egg yolk
pinch of ground coriander
pinch of sugar
60–75 ml/4–5 tablespoons
  sunflower oil
500 g/1 1/4 lb white asparagus
115 g/4 oz rocket
1 lettuce, such as lollo rosso
15 ml/1 tablespoon sunflower seeds
salt and freshly ground white pepper

Approximately per portion:
710 kJ/170 kcal
6 g protein, 16 g fat
4 g carbohydrate

● Approximate preparation
  time: 45 minutes

---

1. Dice the shallots. Mix together the tarragon vinegar, mustard, egg yolk, coriander and sugar and season to taste with salt and pepper. Add the shallots and gradually beat in the oil.

2. Peel the asparagus and cut off the woody ends of the stems. Slice the asparagus diagonally into small chunks. Add them to the dressing and set aside for about 30 minutes.

3. Pull the rocket leaves off their stalks. Finely chop the tender stalks. Tear the lettuce leaves into bite-size pieces.

4. Mix together the salad leaves in a serving bowl, top with the marinated asparagus and sprinkle with the sunflower seeds.

Above: Salad with asparagus and rocket
Below: Fruity fennel salad

Pepper salad with sprouted seeds

Easy • Economical

Serves 4
115 g/4 oz wheat or lentil sprouts
45 ml/3 tablespoons white
*   wine vinegar*
pinch of sugar
60 ml/4 tablespoons olive oil
2 small red peppers
2 small green peppers
2 small yellow peppers
1 courgette, about 200 g/7 oz
130 g/4 1/2 oz cherry tomatoes
2 onions
salt and freshly ground black pepper

Approximately per portion:
795 kJ/190 kcal
10 g protein, 13 g fat
15 g carbohydrate

● Approximate preparation
   time: 40 minutes

---

1. Rinse the wheat sprouts, if using. Briefly blanch the lentil sprouts, if using, in boiling water and drain well.

2. Mix together the vinegar and sugar in a large serving bowl and season with salt and pepper. Gradually beat in the oil.

3. Core and seed the peppers and cut into strips. Halve the courgette lengthways and thinly slice. Halve the tomatoes. Dice the onions. Add the peppers, courgette, tomatoes and onions to the bowl and toss well. Add the sprouts.

Tip

Various sprouts – wheat, lentil, alfalfa – are available from health-food shops and many supermarkets. You can also sprout beans, peas and seeds at home in a large glass jar or a special sprouter.

Endive salad with red lentils

There are two kinds of endive – escarole or broad leaf endive and frisée or curly endive. Escarole may be green or red-tinged. Both types have the characteristic slightly bitter flavour of the chicory family.

Easy • Rather time-consuming

Serves 4
115 g/4 oz red lentils
250 ml/8 fl oz vegetable stock
45 ml/3 tablespoons red
*   wine vinegar*
1 egg yolk
1 clove garlic
75 ml/5 tablespoons oil
1 endive
1 bunch spring onions
salt and freshly ground white pepper

Approximately per portion:
985 kJ/235 kcal
10 g protein, 15 g fat
16 g carbohydrate

● Approximate preparation
   time: 50 minutes

---

1. Put the lentils and stock in a large saucepan, bring to the boil and cook over a high heat for 4–5 minutes.

2. Put the vinegar into a bowl and crush the garlic into it. Mix in the egg yolk and season to taste with salt and pepper. Gradually beat in the oil.

3. Drain the lentils and add them to the mixture. Set aside for about 30 minutes.

4. Tear the endive into bite-size pieces. Thinly slice the spring onions into rings. Add the endive and spring onions to the lentils and mix thoroughly.

Tip

Red lentils do not need to be soaked and their cooking time is only about 4–5 minutes, although sometimes they may require longer. They are good in salads, clear soups and served as a side dish.

Above: Pepper salad with sprouted seeds
Below: Endive salad with red lentils

Crispy salad with grains

Rather time-consuming • Easy

Serves 4
115 g/4 oz mixed whole grains, such
*   as wheat, barley, millet and*
*   oat groats*
250 ml/8 fl oz water
1 onion
60–90 ml/4–6 tablespoons white
*   wine vinegar*
1 egg yolk
10 ml/2 teaspoons medium
*   strong mustard*
pinch of sugar
60 ml/4 tablespoons walnut oil
1 iceberg lettuce
1 cucumber
2 bunches radishes
1/2 bunch celery
salt and freshly ground white pepper

Approximately per portion:
950 kJ/225 kcal
8 g protein, 13 g fat
20 g carbohydrate

● Approximate preparation
   time: 1 1/2 hours

---

1. Put the grain mixture into a saucepan, together with the water. Bring to the boil, cover and simmer over a low heat for about 1 hour, until tender.

2. Finely dice the onion. Mix together the white wine vinegar, egg yolk, mustard and sugar in a large serving bowl and season to taste with salt and pepper. Add the diced onion. Gradually beat in the walnut oil.

3. Add the grains and set aside to cool, stirring from time to time.

4. With a sharp knife, cut the lettuce into bite-size pieces.

5. Cut the cucumber and radishes into matchstick strips. Thinly slice the celery.

6. Add the lettuce, cucumber, radishes and celery to the bowl and mix well. Season to taste with salt and pepper again, if necessary.

Lamb's lettuce with mushrooms

Easy

This makes a delicious starter or a wonderful accompaniment to liver, as well as being a good salad to serve with meat fondues.

Serves 4
250 g/9 oz mushrooms
1 bunch radishes
75 g/3 oz back bacon
4 shallots
45 ml/3 tablespoons oil
60 ml/4 tablespoons white
*   wine vinegar*
400 g/14 oz lamb's lettuce
salt and freshly ground
*   white pepper*

Approximately per portion:
920 kJ/220 kcal
6 g protein, 20 g fat
3 g carbohydrate

● Approximate preparation
   time: 30 minutes

---

1. Thinly slice the mushrooms. Cut the radishes into matchstick strips.

2. Finely dice the bacon. Dry-fry the bacon over a medium heat, stirring constantly, until crisp.

3. Dice the shallots and add them to the frying pan, together with 15 ml/1 tablespoon of the oil. Sauté until the shallots are soft and translucent. Stir in the remaining oil and the vinegar and heat through. Season to taste with salt and pepper.

4. Arrange the lamb's lettuce and mushrooms in a shallow bowl or on a serving plate and pour the lukewarm marinade over them. Sprinkle with the radishes and serve immediately.

Tip

Lamb's lettuce is also known by its French name, mâche. Buy whole plants rather than packed leaves, if possible, as it is quite a fragile plant. Ideally, soak it in iced water for about an hour before using. This freshens the leaves and also helps to clean away sand lodged in the base.

Above: Crispy salad with grains
Below: Lamb's lettuce with mushrooms

Italian fondue with pesto

Exquisite • Rather expensive

Pesto, a sauce made from fresh basil and pine nuts, is a speciality from Liguria, the herb garden of Italy. It is served with vegetable soups and spaghetti. If you cannot obtain fresh basil, use fresh parsley instead. Do not use dried basil.

Serves 4–6
For the pesto:
5 cloves garlic
65 g/2¹/₂ oz pine nuts
1 bunch fresh basil, about
*   50 g/2 oz leaves*
50 g/2 oz Parmesan cheese
120 ml/4 fl oz olive oil
salt
For the fondue:
600 g/1 lb 5 oz boneless, skinless
*   chicken breasts*
juice of 1 lime
8 veal escalopes, each about
*   50 g/2 oz*
2 sprigs fresh sage or 5 ml/
*   1 teaspoon dried sage*
8 thin slices Parma ham
30 ml/2 tablespoons freshly grated
*   Parmesan cheese*
250 g/9 oz calves' liver
750 ml/1¹/₄ pints vegetable oil
salt and freshly ground white pepper

For 6 persons approximately per portion:
2,320 kJ/555 kcal
56 g protein, 35 g fat
3 g carbohydrate

● Approximate preparation time: 1¹/₂ hours

1. Coarsely chop the garlic and the pine nuts. Finely chop the basil leaves.

2. Put the garlic, pine nuts and basil in a large mixing bowl, together with 1.5 ml/¹/₄ teaspoon salt, and beat with a hand-held electric mixer to make a purée. Alternatively, process the mixture in a food processor.

3. Coarsely grate the Parmesan cheese, add it to the bowl and beat it into the mixture. With the motor still running, gradually add the olive oil.

4. Cut the chicken into bite-size cubes. Mix together the lime juice and pepper to taste, add the chicken, tossing to coat well, and set aside to marinate for about 30 minutes.

5. Beat the veal flat with a meat mallet or rolling pin. Sprinkle with salt and pepper to taste and arrange the sage leaves over the meat.

6. Cut the Parma ham in half lengthways and place it on top of the veal. Sprinkle on the Parmesan cheese. Cut the veal escalopes in half lengthways and roll them up. Secure the rolls with the cocktail sticks.

7. Rinse the liver and pat dry with absorbent kitchen paper. Dice into bite-size cubes.

8. Remove the chicken cubes from the marinade, drain well and pat dry with absorbent kitchen paper. Arrange all the meat on serving plates.

9. Heat the oil in a saucepan, pour it into a fondue pan and transfer it to the stand. Adjust the burner so that the oil remains hot, but does not overheat.

10. Spear the meat on fondue forks and fry in the hot oil until crisp and golden brown. Serve with the pesto.

Tip

Other good accompaniments include bottled marinated mushrooms, Anchovy yogurt sauce (see page 34), Crème fraîche with tomato (see page 34), fresh white bread, Italian bread sticks and light white wine.

The cooking of the sunny south has inspired this Italian fondue with pesto. As well as the spicy basil sauce, you should serve at least one other sauce, such as Crème fraîche with tomato.

Puszta Fondue

Easy

Serves 4
400 g/14 oz small firm potatoes
2 brown onions
250 g/9 oz minced beef
1 small egg
30 ml/2 tablespoons breadcrumbs
400 g/14 oz pork fillet
400 g/14 oz Debrecen or chorizo
sausages
2 red peppers
2 green peppers
1 white onion
3 cloves garlic
15 ml/1 tablespoon lard or
vegetable oil
30 ml/2 tablespoons mild paprika
1 litre/1³/4 pints light meat stock
105 ml/7 tablespoons red wine
salt and freshly ground black pepper

Approximately per portion:
3,360 kJ/800 kcal
50 g protein, 55 g fat
21 g carbohydrate

● Approximate preparation
time: 1 hour

1. Put the potatoes in a large saucepan and cover with water. Bring to the boil, cover and simmer over a medium heat for about 20 minutes.

2. Finely dice the brown onions. Knead together half the diced onions with the minced beef, egg, breadcrumbs and salt and pepper to taste.

3. With dampened hands form small meatballs from this mixture and put them on to a plate.

4. Dice the pork fillet into bite-size cubes. Remove the skin from the sausages and cut the sausages into 1 cm/¹/2 inch wide slices.

5. Drain and peel the potatoes, then halve or quarter them, depending on their size.

6. Core and seed the peppers and cut the flesh into chunks. Coarsely dice the white onion.

7. Arrange the meatballs, pork, sausages, potatoes, peppers and white onion on serving plates.

8. Finely chop the garlic. Heat the lard or oil in a large saucepan. Add the remaining diced onions and sauté, stirring frequently, until soft

and translucent. Add the garlic and sauté for 1–2 minutes.

9. Remove the saucepan from the heat and stir in the paprika. Return the pan to the heat and stir in the stock and red wine. Bring to the boil.

10. Transfer the saucepan to a stand. Spear the meat, meatballs and sausages, together with the peppers, white onion and potatoes, in any order you please, on fondue forks and cook them in the stock.

Tip

This fondue goes well with Egg and gherkin smetana (see page 34), Crème fraîche with tomato (see page 34), Cucumber and garlic cheese (see page 38), a green salad with vinaigrette dressing, crusty white bread, red wine or beer.

This fondue has an extraordinary variety of ingredients: meatballs, meat, sausage, potatoes and vegetables. It is served with a spicy sauce, such as Cucumber and garlic cheese.

Mozzarella fondue with tuna mayonnaise

Easy • Quick

Serves 4–6
2 egg yolks
15 ml/1 tablespoon lemon juice
250 ml/8 fl oz olive oil
150 g/5 oz can tuna in brine
150 ml/1/4 pint natural yogurt
15 ml/1 tablespoon capers
750 g/1 lb 10 oz courgettes
500 g/1 1/4 lb mozzarella cheese
2 eggs
90–120 ml/6–8 tablespoons
  fresh breadcrumbs
3/4 litre/1 1/4 pints vegetable oil
1 sprig fresh rosemary or 5 ml/
  1 teaspoon dried rosemary
salt and freshly ground black pepper

**For 6 persons,
approximately per portion:**
2,765 kJ/660 kcal
22 g protein, 54 g fat
16 g carbohydrate

● Approximate preparation
time: 30 minutes

Tip

Good accompaniments include herby crème fraîche, Salad with asparagus and rocket (see page 42), crusty white bread, and a light Italian white wine.

1. Put the egg yolks and lemon juice into a food processor or blender and process. With the motor still running, gradually add the oil until the mixture forms a smooth mayonnaise. Drain the tuna, add it to the mayonnaise and process. Season to taste with salt and pepper and add the capers.

2. Cut the courgettes into 1 cm/ 1/2 inch thick slices. Dice the mozzarella cheese. Beat the eggs in a bowl. Mix the breadcrumbs with salt and pepper to taste in another bowl.

3. Dip the mozzarella cubes first into the egg yolk and then into the breadcrumbs. Arrange them on a serving plate, together with the courgette slices.

4. Heat the oil in a saucepan, pour it into a fondue pan and transfer to the stand. Add the rosemary. Spear the mozzarella and courgettes on fondue forks and fry them in the oil. Serve with the tuna mayonnaise.

Dutch cheese fondue

Easy

Serves 4–6
500 g/1¼ lb chicory
1 medium cauliflower
30 ml/2 tablespoons milk
1 Granary loaf
250 ml/8 fl oz dry white wine
15 ml/1 tablespoon lemon juice
250 g/9 oz medium mature Gouda cheese
250 g/9 oz mild Gouda cheese
15 ml/1 tablespoon cornflour
30 ml/2 tablespoons water
15–30 ml/1–2 tablespoons gin (optional)
salt and freshly ground white pepper

For 6 persons, approximately per portion:
2,660 kJ/635 kcal
32 g protein, 26 g fat
61 g carbohydrate

● Approximate preparation time: 1 hour

Tip

Good accompaniments for this fondue include dill pickles, Crispy Salad with grains (see page 46), lager, white wine spritzer or mineral water.

1. Separate the chicory leaves. Divide the cauliflower into florets and blanch in salted water with the milk for 2–3 minutes. (The milk keeps it white.) Drain in a colander. Dice the bread into bite-size cubes. Arrange the chicory, cauliflower florets and bread separately on serving plates.

2. Bring the white wine and lemon juice to the boil in a ceramic fondue pan. Coarsely grate the cheese and gradually add it to the pan, stirring constantly in figure-of-eight movements with a wooden spoon until the cheese has melted.

3. Mix the cornflour with the water to form a smooth paste and stir it into the cheese fondue. Bring the fondue to the boil, add the gin, if using, and season with pepper. Transfer the fondue to the stand.

4. Spear the cauliflower florets and bread cubes on fondue forks and dip them into the cheese fondue. Hold the chicory leaves at the bottom end and dip them into the cheese fondue.

Thai fondue

Exquisite

Serves 4
400 g/14 oz beef fillet
¹/2 cucumber, about 300 g/11 oz
4 red onions
2 small fresh chillies
75 ml/5 tablespoons vinegar
120 ml/4 fl oz water
60 ml/4 tablespoons brown sugar
3 shallots
2 cloves garlic
130 g/4¹/2 oz roasted,
   unsalted peanuts
250 ml/8 fl oz unsweetened
   coconut milk
pinch of chilli powder
7.5–10 ml/1 1/2–2 teaspoons ground
   coriander
300 g/11 oz skinless, boneless
   chicken breasts
40 g/1¹/2 oz fresh root ginger
2 limes
30 ml/2 tablespoons soy sauce
1.5 litres/2¹/2 pints light
   chicken stock
15 ml/1 tablespoon fresh coriander
   leaves or 5 ml/1 teaspoon dried
salt and freshly ground white pepper
To serve:
sliced mushrooms
shredded Chinese leaves
boiled rice
chilli sauce
soy sauce
green salad

Approximately per portion:
1,890 kJ/455 kcal
47 g protein, 21 g fat
18 g carbohydrate

● Approximate preparation
   time: 3 hours of which
   2 hours are freezing time

---

1. Put the beef fillet in the freezer for about 2 hours.

2. Cut the cucumber in half lengthways and then into thin slices. Cut the onions into thin chunks.

3. Seed the fresh chillies and finely dice the flesh.

4. Put the vinegar, water, sugar and 2.5 ml/¹/2 teaspoon salt in a saucepan and bring to the boil. Add the cucumber, onions and chillies and boil for 3–4 minutes. Remove from the heat and leave them to cool in the liquid.

5. Put the shallots, garlic, peanuts and coconut milk in a food processor and process to a smooth purée.

6. Transfer the peanut sauce to a saucepan and season with chilli powder, half the ground coriander, salt and pepper. Bring the sauce to the boil, stirring constantly. Remove the pan from the heat and set aside to cool completely.

7. Cut the chicken breasts and beef fillet into very thin slices.

8. Peel and grate the ginger. Finely grate the lime rind and set aside. Squeeze the lime juice. Mix the lime juice with the ginger, the remaining ground coriander and the soy sauce. Pour this over the meat, turning to coat, and set aside to marinate for 1 hour, stirring frequently.

9. Arrange the meat on a serving plate. Bring the chicken stock to the boil in a large saucepan and

add the lime rind. Transfer the saucepan to a stand or pour the stock into a Chinese 'fire-pot' and place on the stand. Add the fresh or dried coriander.

10. Spear the meat on fondue forks or put it into fondue scoops and cook it in the stock. Serve with the cucumber and onion pickle and the peanut sauce and sliced mushrooms, shredded Chinese leaves, rice, chilli sauce, soy sauce, a green salad, light beer, dry white wine or jasmine tea.

Tip

It is important to use unsweetened coconut milk for the peanut sauce. If you would like to prepare this yourself, put 115 g/4 oz grated coconut, 250 ml/8 fl oz milk and 250 ml/8 fl oz water in a saucepan, bring to the boil and simmer for about 5 minutes. Strain and measure out the required amount.

This is the way they serve a fondue in Asia. If possible, it should be cooked in a traditional Asian 'fire-pot' and served with spicy peanut sauce and cucumber and onion pickle.

Andalusian fondue

Easy

Serves 4–6
500 g/1 1/4 lb chicken livers
30 ml/2 tablespoons medium
  dry sherry
4–6 cloves garlic
250 ml/8 fl oz mayonnaise
150 g/5 oz small shallots
450 g/1 lb back bacon,
  rinds removed
200 g/7 oz prunes, stoned
2 x 250 g/9 oz cans artichoke
  hearts
750 ml/1 1/4 pints vegetable oil
salt and freshly ground
  black pepper
To serve:
chilli sauce
olives
crusty white bread

**For 6 persons,
approximately per portion:**
4,145 kJ/990 kcal
28 g protein, 75 g fat
33 g carbohydrate

● Approximate preparation
  time: 1 hour

---

1. Rinse the chicken livers and pat dry with absorbent kitchen paper. Cut them into bite-size pieces. Season to taste with pepper and sprinkle them with the sherry. Set aside to marinate for about 30 minutes.

2. Crush the garlic and stir it into the mayonnaise. Season to taste with salt and pepper.

3. Briefly blanch the shallots in boiling water and rinse them in cold water. Remove the skins.

4. Cut the bacon slices in half across. Wrap each shallot and each prune in 1 piece of bacon and secure with a cocktail stick.

5. Cut the artichoke hearts into quarters. Wrap each of the artichoke quarters and chicken livers in 1 piece of bacon and secure with a cocktail stick.

6. Heat the oil. Pour it into a fondue pan and transfer it to the stand. Spear the little parcels on fondue forks and fry them in the oil, then dip them in the mayonnaise.

7. Serve with chilli sauce, olives, crusty white bread and a robust red wine.

Cheddar cheese fondue

Easy

Serves 4
1 bunch celery
1 large white loaf
250 ml/8 fl oz dry white wine
10 ml/2 teaspoons
  lemon juice
500 g/1 1/4 lb Cheddar cheese
15 ml/1 tablespoon cornflour
45 ml/3 tablespoons water
1 bunch fresh mint or 10 ml/
  2 teaspoons dried mint
freshly ground white pepper
To serve:
mixed pickles
sweetcorn
cocktail onions

Approximately per portion:
3,560 kJ/850 kcal
43 g protein, 43 g fat
63 g carbohydrate

● Approximate preparation
  time: 45 minutes

---

1. Cut the celery into 2.5 cm/ 1 inch chunks. Dice the bread into bite-size cubes. Arrange both separately on serving plates.

2. Bring the white wine and lemon juice to the boil in a ceramic fondue pan.

3. Coarsely grate the cheese and gradually add it to the pan, stirring constantly in figure-of-eight movements with a wooden spoon until the cheese has melted.

4. Mix together the cornflour and water to a smooth paste and add it to the cheese fondue. Bring to the boil, stirring constantly, and season to taste with pepper.

5. Chop the mint leaves and stir them into the cheese fondue. Transfer the fondue to the stand.

6. Spear the bread cubes and celery on fondue forks and dip them into the cheese fondue. Serve with mixed pickles, sweetcorn, cocktail onions, beer or Guinness.

Above: Andalusian fondue
Below: Cheddar cheese fondue

Caribbean fondue

Exquisite • Rather time-consuming

Serves 4
600 g/1 lb 5 oz boneless, skinless
    chicken breasts
250 g/9 oz pork fillet
250 g/9 oz peeled raw prawns
2 limes
4 cloves garlic
1 fresh green chilli
30 ml/2 tablespoons dark rum
2 plantains
2 red peppers
2 green peppers
750 ml/1 1/4 pints peanut oil
To serve:
mango chutney
Avocado dip (see page 36)
Cranberry and onion sauce (see
    page 38)
fresh mango slices
fresh pineapple cubes

Approximately per portion:
2,070 kJ/495 kcal
60 g protein, 11 g fat
13 g carbohydrate

● Approximate preparation
   time: 6 1/2 hours of which
   6 hours are marinating time

---

1. Dice the meat into small cubes and put it into a shallow bowl. Place the prawns in another bowl.

2. Grate the lime rinds and squeeze the juice. Finely dice the garlic. Seed and finely dice the chilli. Mix together the lime rind, lime juice, garlic, chilli and rum.

3. Pour the marinade over the meat and over the prawns and toss to coat. Set aside to marinate for about 6 hours.

4. Peel and thinly slice the plantains and arrange the slices on a plate. Core and seed the peppers. Cut the flesh into 2 cm/3/4 inch cubes and arrange them on a plate.

5. Pat the meat and prawns dry with kitchen paper and arrange on a plate.

6. Heat the oil in a saucepan, pour it into a fondue pan and transfer it to the stand. Spear the meat, prawns, plantain slices and diced peppers on fondue forks and fry them in the hot oil until crisp. Serve with mango chutney, Avocado dip, Cranberry and onion sauce, fresh mango slices, fresh pineapple cubes, white wine or beer.

Tip

Indulge yourself by serving a bowl of exotic fruits, such as pineapples, mangoes, pomegranates and lychees. You can either put the fruits into the fondue or serve them as a dessert with a scoop of ice cream. Banana leaves and flowers look pretty as table decorations.

This exotic fondue with chicken, pork and prawns, marinated in a slightly hot sauce, is delicious served with tropical fruit.

Turkey and beef fondue

Easy

Serves 4
1 onion
250 ml/8 fl oz mayonnaise
juice of 1 lime
45 ml/3 tablespoons Cumberland
* sauce*
75 ml/5 tablespoons tomato
* ketchup*
15 ml/1 tablespoon brandy
* (optional)*
500 g/1 1/4 lb turkey breast fillet
300 g/11 oz loin of beef
lettuce leaves
325 g/11 1/2 oz can corn cobs
750 ml/1 1/4 pints vegetable oil
salt and freshly ground white pepper

Approximately per portion:
3,475 kJ/830 kcal
50 g protein, 44 g fat
33 g carbohydrate

● Approximate preparation
  time: 50 minutes

---

1. Finely dice the onion. Mix together the mayonnaise, lime juice, Cumberland sauce, tomato ketchup and diced onion. Season to taste with salt and pepper and stir in the brandy, if using.

2. Dice the turkey and beef into bite-size cubes and arrange them on a bed of lettuce leaves on serving plates.

3. Drain the corn cobs and, if large, cut into 2 cm/3/4 inch slices. Arrange them on a plate.

4. Heat the oil in a saucepan, pour it into a fondue pan and transfer to the stand. Spear the meat and corn cobs on fondue forks and fry them in the hot oil. Serve with the ketchup mayonnaise.

Tip

This fondue goes well with herb butter, Roquefort cream (see page 36), Tomato chutney (see page 40), crusty white bread and red wine.

Greek fondue

Rather time-consuming

This delicious fondue is full of the sunshine flavours of the Mediterranean, especially if you can obtain fresh herbs.

Serves 4
600 g/1 lb 5 oz boneless lamb
250 g/9 oz boneless pork
6 cloves garlic
45 ml/3 tablespoons olive oil
5 ml/1 teaspoon coarsely
* ground pepper*
8 sprigs fresh marjoram or 5 ml/
* 1 teaspoon dried marjoram*
500 g/1 1/4 lb courgettes
2 bunches spring onions
750 ml/1 1/4 pints vegetable oil
To serve:
chillies
Cucumber and garlic cheese
* (see page 38)*
Tomato chutney (see page 40)
Lamb's lettuce with mushrooms
* (see page 46)*
pitta bread

Approximately per portion:
3,130 kJ/750 kcal
41 g protein, 50 g fat
6 g carbohydrate

● Approximate preparation
  time: 6 1/2 hours of which
  6 hours are marinating time

---

1. Dice the lamb and pork into bite-size cubes.

2. Finely dice the garlic. Mix together the olive oil, pepper and garlic. If using fresh marjoram, pull the leaves off the stems. Mix the marjoram with the oil.

3. Pour the marinade over the meat and turn to coat. Set aside to marinate for about 6 hours.

4. Cut the courgettes in half lengthways and then into 1 cm/1/2 inch chunks. Cut the spring onions into 2.5 cm/1 inch pieces. Arrange the courgettes and spring onions on a plate.

5. Remove the meat from the marinade, drain and pat dry with kitchen paper. Arrange it on a plate.

6. Heat the oil in a saucepan, pour it into a fondue pan and transfer it to the stand. As their cooking times are different – the vegetables cook faster than the meat – spear the meat and vegetables on separate fondue forks and fry in the hot oil. Serve with chillies, Cucumber and garlic cheese, Tomato chutney, Lamb's lettuce with mushrooms, pitta bread, beer or retsina.

Above: Turkey and beef fondue
Below: Greek fondue

Great Little Cook Books
Fondues

Published originally under the title
Fondues by Gräfe und Unzer Verlag
GmbH, München

© 1992 by Gräfe und Unzer Verlag
GmbH, München

English-language edition
© 1999 by Transedition Limited,
Oxford, England

This edition published by
Aura Books plc

Translation:
Translate-A-Book, Oxford

Editing:
Linda Doeser

Typesetting:
Organ Graphic, Abingdon

10 9 8 7 6 5 4 3 2 1
Printed in Dubai

ISBN 1 901683 37 0

On the front cover you
can see Caribbean fondue
(recipe on page 58).

Important information
Cooking at the table requires a
heat source – spirit burner, fuel
paste, gas, electricity – which must
be securely set up and carefully
watched. The contents of the
fondue pan, whether cheese, oil or
stock, can also become
dangerously hot and may even
spurt out. It is, therefore, most
important that you never leave an
unattended fondue on the table.
Special care must be taken if there
are children present. Do not go in
for false economy when you buy
your fondue equipment. The
burner and the pan must stand
steadily and, if possible, they should
have a spray guard and conform
with general safety requirements.
Never heat oil or stock in an
earthenware caquelon, which is
designed for cheese fondues, as
the heat can break it.

Note:
Quantities for all recipes are given
in both metric and imperial
measures and, if appropriate, in
standard measuring spoons. They
are not interchangeable, so readers
should follow one set or the other.
5 ml = 1 teaspoon
15 ml = 1 tablespoon

Antje Grüner
has been concerned with nutrition
for more than twenty years – in
theory and practice. A long stay
abroad made her acquainted with
international cookery. She was
editor of various well-known
specialist journals and translated
her experiences into words and
pictures. Now she works as a
freelance food journalist and
cookery writer.

Odette Teubner
was taught by her father, the
internationally renowned food
photographer, Christian Teubner.
At present, she works exclusively
in the Teubner Studio for Food
Photography. In her spare time she
is an enthusiastic painter of
children's portraits. She uses her
own son as a model.

Kerstin Mosny
studied photography at a college in
French-speaking Switzerland. After
that she worked as an assistant to
various photographers, including
the food photographer, Jürgen
Tapprich in Zürich. She now works
in the Teubner Studio for Food
Photography.